# TABLE

## Communion Meditations

Compiled by

## Pat Fittro

STANDARD
PUBLISHING
Cincinnati, Ohio

Meditations taken from *The Christian Standard*.

**Library of Congress Cataloging-in-Publication Data**

At His table : communion meditations / compiled by Pat Fittro.
     p.     cm.
  ISBN 0-7847-0464-3
  1. Lord's Supper—Meditations.    I. Fittro, Pat
BV826.5.A7    1996
242—dc20
                           96-3878
                            CIP

The Standard Publishing Company, Cincinnati, Ohio
A division of Standex International Corporation
© 1996 by The Standard Publishing Company
All rights reserved
Printed in the United States of America

03 02 01 00 99 98 97 96          5 4 3 2 1

# Contents

| | | |
|---|---|---|
| My Fair Share | Psalm 103:10-12 | 5 |
| Be Reconciled | Matthew 5:23, 24 | 7 |
| According to Code | Matthew 7:24, 25 | 9 |
| Common Everyday Things | | |
| | Matthew 26:17-29 | 11 |
| Completed Meal | Mark 14:22-25 | 13 |
| Our Place Setting | Luke 14:1-11 | 15 |
| Words to Hang Onto | Luke 19:45-48 | 17 |
| A Celebration | Luke 22:15 | 19 |
| Meeting the Moment | Luke 22:17-22 | 21 |
| Seeking God | Luke 22:19, 20 | 24 |
| A Remembrance | Luke 22:19 | 27 |
| Do This in Remembrance of Me | | |
| | Luke 22:19 | 29 |
| What's for Dinner? | Luke 22:19, 20 | 31 |
| Time of Renewal | Luke 22:14-30 | 33 |
| Remember Me | Luke 23:42 | 35 |
| I Love You | John 3:16, 17 | 37 |
| Spiritual Feast | John 6:48-51 | 39 |
| Facets of a Diamond | John 6:53-56 | 41 |
| Weekly and Weakly | John 14:15-21 | 43 |
| Forgetting the Anguish Because of the Joy | | |
| | John 16:20-22 | 45 |
| Much in Common | Acts 2:42-46 | 47 |
| The Unifying Power of the Blood | | |
| | Acts 17:26 | 49 |
| Christ Died for Us | Romans 5:7-9 | 51 |
| Unity | 1 Corinthians 11:20-29 | 53 |
| Let Us Remember | 1 Corinthians 11:23-26 | 55 |
| A Memorial | 1 Corinthians 11:23-26 | 57 |

| We Thank You | 1 Corinthians 11:24-26 | 59 |
| Solemn Joy | 1 Corinthians 11:26 | 61 |
| Until He Comes | 1 Corinthians 11:26 | 63 |
| A Time to Replenish | 1 Corinthians 11:26 | 65 |
| Self-Examination | 1 Corinthians 11:28 | 67 |
| Christ's Healing | Galatians 2:20 | 69 |
| Both Sides of the Cross | Ephesians 2:11-22 | 71 |
| Forgiveness | Philippians 2:5-8 | 73 |
| To Him All Majesty Ascribe | | |
| | Philippians 2:8-11 | 75 |
| "If It's Broken, Fix It" | Hebrews 4:15, 16 | 77 |
| Hope | Hebrews 6:11, 19 | 79 |
| Free | 1 Peter 1:13 | 81 |
| The Threefold Look | Revelation 22:20 | 83 |

**SPECIAL DAYS**

| New Year | 2 Peter 1:19-21 | 85 |
| Everything Old Is New Again | | |
| | Hebrews 9:15 | 87 |
| Tell Me Again, Lord | Luke 22:19 | 89 |
| Out of Darkness | Matthew 27:45-54 | 91 |
| In Remembrance | 1 Corinthians 11:24 | 93 |
| Mother's Day | John 19:25-27 | 95 |
| In Memoriam | John 6:53-58 | 97 |
| A Memorial Day Meditation | | |
| | John 10:25-30 | 98 |
| Daddy! You're Home | Romans 8:15 | 101 |
| Miss Liberty | Matthew 1:21 | 103 |
| Labor Day | 1 Corinthians 11:23-26 | 105 |
| Thanksgiving | 1 Corinthians 11:23-26 | 107 |
| Christmas Meditation | Matthew 26:26-29 | 109 |
| Did Joseph Know? | Matthew 1:18-24 | 111 |

# My Fair Share

*Psalm 103:10-12*

Sometimes we say, "All I want is my fair share. All I want is what's coming to me." We all want to be treated fairly, don't we? We all want the proper change back when we buy something. If we find we have been shortchanged and didn't get what was coming to us, we become angry. We vehemently demand our rights.

There is one area where I am glad we don't get a square deal and a fair shake. It is an area where I will never demand my rights and insist on what's coming to me. It is an area where I will forever remain silent and simply be thankful that I got shortchanged. The area of which I speak is our sin.

"He does not treat us as our sins deserve or repay us according to our iniquities. For as high as the heavens are above the earth, so great is his love for those who fear him; as far as the east is from the west, so far has he removed our transgressions from us" (Psalm 103:10-12).

God does not treat us as our sins required or as we deserved. Our sins were deserving of punishment. Instead, we received reward. We deserved death, but in its place we received life. The one who deserved glory accepted our guilt. Jesus took our sins upon himself.

Why? Love! Measureless love that knows no limits was the reason. How far do the heavens reach? The heavens extend for untold millions of miles. If we can understand the limits of our universe, then we can understand God's love for us. I don't understand it, but I'm thankful for it.

Our sins have been removed from our lives never to be remembered again. When you travel toward the western horizon from the east, you never reach it. It simply stretches on before you. As far as the east is from the west, that is how far our sins are from us.

Jesus made this possible. We remember these facts by participating in the Lord's Supper. May we honor the one who made it possible for us to get what we didn't deserve—forgiveness and eternal life.

—David McConnell
Poseyville, Indiana

Date used: _____

# Be Reconciled

*Matthew 5:23, 24*

Though it has been almost fifteen years, the words still sting my heart as if they had been spoken only five minutes ago. "I will never forgive you. I am so deeply hurt that I will never be able to forgive you. I hate you."

How often those words are spoken! Husbands say them to wives. Wives to husbands. Parents to children. And all too often they are said Christian to Christian.

Currently, I am aware of a major rift that exists between two families in the same church. Both parties are hurt. They are angry. They say that the wall that separates them is so high . . . and insurmountable. No doubt you've seen it too.

Have we forgotten what the Lord has done for us? Are we so accustomed to His grace that we fail to remember just how much He has forgiven us?

As we partake of Communion today, our

faith in Christ becomes very, very practical. Yes, we do this in remembrance of Him. That remembrance ought to cause us to:

• Go and be reconciled with our brother when we come before the Lord to be reconciled to Him (Matthew 5:23, 24).
• "Accept one another, then, just as Christ accepted you, in order to bring praise to God" (Romans 15:7).

As we partake of the body and the blood of Jesus today, may we see that it is possible for us to forgive. It may be difficult for us. It may be painful, but it is possible. May we also see that we dare not hold on to our own personal hurts and offenses, but realize that we lost the right to refuse to forgive at the foot of the cross.

—Buddy Reed
Fayetteville, North Carolina

Date used: _____

# According to Code

*Matthew 7:24, 25*

The devastation of Hurricane Andrew was nearly complete in south Florida. However, one house stood tall in the midst of the debris, almost as if nothing had happened.

The owner was asked why his house had escaped destruction when others around his had not escaped. He stated that he had built it himself and that he had followed to the letter the instructions from the building code manual. It was supposed to withstand the force of a hurricane.

When Jesus said, "This do in remembrance of me," was He not giving instruction whereby we might, as Christians, stand firm in the midst of a raging storm? Would not our doing so be akin to the wise man who built his house upon a rock?

We need to heed Jesus' instructions when we approach the table. God's building code manual, the Bible, provides us with what we need in order to come to His table. It stands firm even in the midst of raging spiritual storms.

—Richard Throckmorton
Veedersburg, Indiana

Date used: _____

# Common Everyday Things

*Matthew 26:17-29*

There are many types of Bibles in our world today. I have one that is special to me, a very old one dating back to the 1860s.

Common, everyday things sometimes take on special meanings. A handshake becomes significant when it brings two enemies together as friends. A kiss symbolizes love and commitment. A letter becomes a treasure when it is the last one from a loved one.

In similar fashion, Jesus took common, ordinary elements—unleavened bread and the fruit of the vine—and made them special. These elements are part of the Passover meal even today. They are easily accessible, inexpensive, and simple. But to the Christian, the loaf and the cup will always be meaningful and special.

They remind us of the broken body and shed blood of our Lord and Savior. He captivates our will, so that we can respond to His will. He enters our minds, so we can think His thoughts. He is faithful to His promises. He died as a sacrifice for our sins.

One can imagine how thrilled the early Christians were to meet together about the Lord's table on the first day of the week. In Matthew 26:26, we read, "Jesus took bread, gave thanks and broke it, and gave it to his disciples, saying 'Take and eat; this is my body.' Then he took the cup, gave thanks, and offered it to them, saying, 'Drink from it, all of you. This is my blood of the covenant, which is poured out for many for the forgiveness of sins.'" He also said, "Do this in remembrance of me."

This kept the memory of Christ alive for many early Christians, and it still does today, for Christians everywhere.

—Don Vollmuth
Dublin, Ohio

Date used: _____

# Completed Meal

*Mark 14:22-25*

"While they were eating, Jesus took bread, gave thanks and broke it, and gave it to his disciples, saying, 'Take it; this is my body.' Then he took the cup, gave thanks and offered it to them, and they all drank from it. 'This is my blood of the covenant, which is poured out for many,' he said to them. 'I tell you the truth, I will not drink again of the fruit of the vine until that day when I drink it anew in the kingdom of God'" (Mark 14:22-25).

The Passover meal had progressed to a point where Jesus interjected this very familiar scene. Breaking the bread, He likened it to His body. The cup, He said, is His "blood of the covenant."

At that very moment Jesus did an extraordinary thing. He propelled the Passover meal or the "Last Supper" into a perpetual future event. Although that meal was likely not meant to end at that time, Jesus abruptly ended it by saying, "I tell you the truth, I will not drink again of the fruit of the vine until that day when I drink it anew in the kingdom of God."

An act which is never finished is ever-present. It lingers on and on, never reaching a conclusion or finding complete resolution. In 1 Corinthians 11:24 Paul adds that when we eat and drink at the Lord's table, we should do so in "remembrance" of Jesus.

We remember Jesus and the Lord's Supper not only in what He has already done in the work of salvation, but in what He is going to do when He finally brings that meal to a conclusion.

Each time we eat and drink that meal we should be in a constant state of readiness looking forward to finally being with Him and all those who have claimed Him and His salvation, as He stands at the head of the table of the wedding supper (Revelation 19:9). There He will raise the cup of the fruit of the vine, and invite each of us to drink with Him together as that meal is finally concluded.

In this way we are not only sharing with Him continually in the drinking of a cup which is His "blood of the covenant," but are constantly looking forward to sharing with Him His final victory, remembering His sacrifice for each of us.

—James B. Killebrew
Lincoln, Illinois

Date used: _____

# Our Place Setting

*Luke 14:1-11*

In our house my father always sat in the same place. When I was a child, I usually sat in the same place too. But our place at the table was really not that important.

During biblical times, however, the place where you sat at the dinner table was very important. In some houses you would find a raised platform for the upper table. This is where the honored guests would sit (Matthew 23:6). The honored guest would sit at the right of the host and the second most honored guest at the left. The honored guest would always get the best plate of food and the biggest portion.

Christ tells the parable of the guests (Luke 14) when He is invited to eat at the house of one of the leaders of the Pharisees. Christ probably saw how, as the guests entered the house, they were pushing and shoving to find a place to sit where they would be most honored. Christ said, "For everyone who exalts himself will be humbled, and he who humbles himself will be exalted" (Luke 14:11).

Christ points out a life-changing point. To lead, you must serve. To be rich, you must be poor. To be exalted, you must be humbled. As we assemble around the Lord's table, it is time for us to let go of self and focus on God. Let us lay aside our foolish pride and humble ourselves before His throne where He has saved us a seat.

—Derrick Horne
Tulsa, Oklahoma

Date used: _____

# Words to Hang Onto

*Luke 19:45-48*

Luke 19:45-48 tells how Jesus drove out merchants who were selling in the temple area. The account continues telling about Jesus teaching every day, and the desire of the Jewish leaders to kill Him. But they could not find a way to do it "because all the people hung on his words."

"All the people hung on his words." I find that an extremely interesting phrase. Simply, the people were following Jesus, listening to His preaching, watching His miracles being performed. They were clinging to His words.

Jesus' words are indeed life-giving. We don't hear them directly from His lips. Fortunately, though, we have them recorded in the Bible. They are there for His people, His followers, today. They are recorded for us to hang onto.

And these words of life we share with

others: "I am the bread of life"; "I am the way, the truth, and the life"; "I am the vine and you are the branches." Jesus said that the person who hears His words and puts them into practice is like the man who built his house by laying the foundation on rock—a strong house that would withstand all types of inclemencies (Luke 6:46-49).

Jesus' words are words of life—words for us to hang onto.

—Howard O. Ross
Baltimore, Maryland

Date used: _____

# A Celebration

*Luke 22:15*

Communion—it's a love feast—with me seated in front of Your table, while You give me Your food: I feed off Your meat and drink.

And it's a celebration—of us being together, because You are so happy, like You were the first night You inaugurated this commemoration. It's a celebration of my participation in Your life—of Your sharing with me, of us eating together, of me eating with the members of Your body, of us communing together.

This is so enjoyable—because You spread a table before me, even in the presence of my enemies. I drink the wine of forgiveness because it is the wine of forgetfulness of other's faults. You enjoy seeing Your members eating Your meal, because giving is what You do. Oh, let me participate in that communion of Your qualities! This is the high and real communion—to partake of

Your nature, like drinking water from a fountain warmed by Your light.

You hold out the cup to me, requesting me to drink. And I do so, because I need to drink in Your mind in order to live. "Come to the waters" (Isaiah 55:1), is Your call for communion. You want us to enjoy Your table together while You fill the whole room with light.

—Camilia Belcher
Belcher, Kentucky

Date used: _____

# Meeting the Moment

*Luke 22:17-22*

Seated around Him at the table, their eyes still veiled to His identity, they clung to His words like orphans at the cloak of a visitor. They may have not, that night, noticed the plainness of His features or the commonness of His clothing for He had succeeded in making their hunger complete.

They had seen His compassion with so many. With a touch a blind man saw; with a word the dead arose. His gentleness He wore with humility when the children of Israel delighted in His presence. His forgiveness extended not only to the rebellious and wayfaring but also even to those who thought themselves to be among God's chosen.

As He walked amidst His own creation, He gave because giving was the very essence of His nature. It was said of Him that He would not break a bruised reed or snuff

21

out a smoldering wick but, instead, would brace the reed and rekindle the flame.

These men with Him, while not fully understanding, had, in faith, chosen to follow Him where He might lead. And by His loving, He had caused each to examine himself to see into the depths of poverty of the human spirit apart from God. He led them to this moment, into His final act of sacrifice in a life dignified by sacrifice.

"This is my body, given for you ... "

He was a gentle, caring man, who was stripped and beaten, spiked to a piece of wood and speared deep in His side. He hung, transfixed in pain, on a lonely hill.

"This is my blood of the covenant, which is poured out for many ... " (Matthew 26:28).

He is the compassionate, loving Father, stretching out His arms to gather His children to safety, who stood in silence while being despised and ridiculed by men full of treachery against Him.

Yet still, in His dying, as He suffered for our rebellion, His love reached out to meet the moment: "Father, forgive them, for they do not know what they are doing" (Luke 23:34).

Today as we remember our Lord's sacrifice we are now before Him from so many walks of life. Some are here with astonishing faith and do not know it. The rest of us, whose faith could not move a mustard seed, let alone a mountain, come like so many bruised reeds and smoldering wicks as we approach His presence. We do not see clearly to have enough love to meet the moment as our Lord did. We see the broken and avert our eyes. We hear the dying and cannot move to touch their heads with tenderness. These are among us even now. As we remember His example, may He grant us gentleness and compassion that we may reach out for the lost and lonely as He has shown us.

—Gregory E. Morrell
Joplin, Missouri

Date used: _____

# Seeking God

*Luke 22:19, 20*

Each of us has come seeking God. In many other buildings, in many other places, many other people are also seeking God. Many more are seeking, but do not know where to look.

The events of the past year—earthquakes, bitter cold and wind, floods and other natural disasters—give us pause. We know that God is powerful, and we wonder how we can approach such a powerful God. How does God manifest himself to His people? Should we seek Him only in the overpowering physical events as those we have witnessed?

Consider the experience of Elijah:

"The Lord said, 'Go out and stand on the mountain in the presence of the Lord, for the Lord is about to pass by.' Then a great and powerful wind tore the mountains apart and shattered the rocks before the Lord, but the

Lord was not in the wind. After the wind there was an earthquake, but the Lord was not in the earthquake. After the earthquake came a fire, but the Lord was not in the fire. And after the fire came a gentle whisper. When Elijah heard it, he pulled his cloak over his face and went out and stood at the mouth of the cave. Then a voice said to him, 'What are you doing here, Elijah?'" (1 Kings 19: 11-13)

God was not in the wind, the earthquake, or the fire. He spoke to His servant in a whisper.

Think about how God made himself known through Jesus.

When the storm arose on the sea, Jesus was not in the wind. He was in the boat with the disciples. He calmed the wind.

When James and John wanted to call down fire from Heaven on the Samaritan village, He rebuked them. He would not be a part of the fire.

When on that fateful Friday afternoon that an earthquake shook Jerusalem so violently that the tombs were broken open and the dead walked about, where was Jesus? He was on the cross, paying the price for our sins.

I really don't know if the disciples ever compared their experiences of wind, fire, and earthquake, with that of Elijah. But I do know that they remembered their encounter with God in the flesh in a quiet upper room:

"And he took bread, gave thanks and broke it, and gave it to them, saying, 'This is my body given for you; do this in remembrance of me.' In the same way, after the supper he took the cup, saying, 'This cup is the new covenant in my blood, which is poured out for you'" (Luke 22:19, 20).

Jesus wanted us to do this in remembrance of Him. If we seek Him, we are assured that we will find Him here, at this feast of remembrance.

—Ken Akins, Jr.
Atlanta, Georgia

Date used: _____

# A Remembrance

*Luke 22:19*

Almost everyone has "things" that they keep to remind them of good times, good friends, or other positive things.

I have my Dad's pocket watch and ring that were given to me at his death to remember him. The value of these things as remembrances pertain only to me. To the rest of the world, their value is established by their resale value.

Jesus knew that we would tend to forget Him and His teachings, when we were left alone. So He arranged to leave us something to remember Him. Jesus knew that the reminder must be simple and easy to obtain. When He selected the bread and fruit of the vine to become His body and blood, He found something that was available to all Christians worldwide.

In His instructions on how to partake, He said, "This is my body given for you; do this in remembrance of me" (Luke 22:19).

This remembrance is not an individual thing like my Dad's watch and ring. It can mean the same to every Christian in the world. It is not focused entirely on the past like my Dad's watch and ring, and it has no resale value. This remembrance is focused on Jesus' risen body and blood. It represents the fulfillment of God's promise of eternal life.

We should always remember Jesus' love for us, as individuals. He cared enough to leave a remembrance that would be common to all of us.

—Robert C. Miller
Bartlesville, Oklahoma

Date used: _____

# Do This in Remembrance of Me

*Luke 22:19*

Each time we meet around the Lord's table, we should do so with the expectation of meeting our Lord and Savior, Jesus Christ. We need to meet in a way that we feel His "holy" presence. We need to leave the table feeling refreshed in our spirit, have our spiritual "gas-tank" filled so we can meet the unspiritual world face-to-face come Monday morning. We need to satisfy our spiritual hungers.

Let us meet around His table with clean, pure hearts that have been cleansed with the shed blood of Christ on Calvary's cross.

To meet in His remembrance, we must lay aside all those things that separate us from the love of God and Jesus Christ. A sure self-examination would be a practicing "fruit of the Spirit" Christian.

The next time we meet in His remembrance, may we do so with the attitude, "I surrender my all to the one who surrendered His all for us on Calvary's cross." Might we take comfort knowing that the spirit of Christ comes with stretched, nail-pierced hands beckoning, "Come unto me and I will give you rest." May the words of Christ, "Do this in remembrance of me," take on a new meaning each time we meet around His table.

—Clyde E. Shearer
Eustis, Florida

Date used: _____

# What's for Dinner?

*Luke 22:19, 20*

Picture this scene: the disciples and Jesus have just partaken of the Passover meal. Jesus said, "This is my body given for you; do this in remembrance of me. . . . This cup is the new covenant in my blood, which is poured out for you."

The disciples were probably wondering what Jesus was talking about. This was the most important meal the disciples had ever shared with Jesus, but they did not even realize it. Still reclined around the table, Jesus explained to them that one of these apostles would betray the Son of Man. How did the disciples react to this statement? They had an argument about who is the greatest.

In many ways, we are like the apostles. During the Lord's Supper, we allow our minds to wander. We think about petty things. The Lord's Supper is a time when we come together and remember what Christ did for us on Calvary. How can we acknowledge Him in a deeper, more personal way? Here are some suggestions:

1. Prepare yourself the night before. Read a passage of Scripture about the Lord's Supper and meditate on it. Thank God for sending Jesus. Pray that we keep focused on Him.

2. During the Lord's Supper, keep your mind free of distractions. While the Communion is being served, you might read Psalm 22, a prophecy that Jesus fulfilled at the cross; or Psalm 32, a song of praise to the Lord.

We all need to examine ourselves during the Lord's Supper. Are we truly concentrating on the cross, or are we like the disciples who were busy with petty things?

—Jennifer Osterholz
Joplin, Missouri

Date used: _____

# Time of Renewal

*Luke 22:14-30*

This passage records the saddest days of history. With the help of Judas, the religious leaders were about to complete their plot to kill the most enlightened man in their nation. But these days were the greatest for Jesus. He was about to complete the mission that His Father had sent Him to perform. He confirmed to His disciples that they would continue His mission.

It is interesting to me that Jesus instituted His new Passover in the midst of human weakness, failure, and pride. Today it is no different. We come around this table this morning ready to commune with Jesus. To this table we bring all of our failures and weaknesses.

I am glad that the Lord doesn't require perfection before one can partake of this cup and loaf. If that were the case we would have to leave them covered and continue on with our service. But because of God's mercy and grace, Jesus still says, "I have eagerly desired to eat this Passover with you."

So we come with our pride, our hatred, our conceit, our slander, our sins—knowing that in repentance we can find forgiveness.

Come partake of this cup and loaf with our perfect Savior. Remember Jesus and His sacrifice. Let this be a time of renewal to your soul.

—Don Kelley
Marion, Ohio

Date used: _____

# Remember Me

*Luke 23:42*

The thief on the cross said, "Jesus, remember me when you come into your kingdom" (Luke 23:42). We regularly say the same thing to Jesus: "Remember me now that You are with God in Heaven." We want Jesus to be always mindful of us—our hurts, pains, desires, afflictions, uncertainties, and fears. We want Him to "pay attention" to us, bail us out of our difficulties, and solve our problems.

Jesus said, "Remember me when you eat this bread and drink this fruit of the vine" (paraphrase of Luke 22:19, 20). Are we as faithful and fervent in remembering Jesus as we are in wanting Him to remember us?

Do we comprehend what He did for us and pay homage to Him with our minds, hearts, and memories? With our love and obedience? Are we diligent in meeting Him at His table each first day of the week?

Why should I expect Jesus to "remember me" if I do not remember Him? He gave us a special ordinance so we can remember Him regularly. He gave us objects—the bread and the juice—to help us remember His body which He willingly subjected to being killed for us, and His blood which He compassionately poured out for us. He wants us to remember what He did—for you and me. He carried our sins to the cross so that we can live victoriously with Him on this earth and forever with Him in Heaven. What gratitude and love such remembering should evoke from us!

At His table I do remember Him and His indescribable gift to me. Throughout the week I continue that remembering through my obedience to Him. And Jesus answers, "Today you will be with me in paradise." and "I am with you always." Remember Jesus!

— Carolyn Dobbs
Indianapolis, Indiana

Date used: _____

# I Love You

*John 3:16, 17*

John 3:16, 17 says this: "For God so loved the world that he gave his one and only Son, that whoever believes in him shall not perish but have eternal life. For God did not send his Son into the world to condemn the world, but to save the world through him."

From the creation of the world, to the beautiful Garden of Eden, God was shouting, "I love you!"

From the freeing of the Israelites from Egypt, to their entering into the Promised Land, God was shouting, "I love you!"

From an animal's feeding trough, called a manger, in the little town of Bethlehem, wherein lay God's own Son, God was shouting, "I love you!"

From the cross of Calvary, where Jesus hung, suffering, bleeding, and dying for the sins of the world, God was shouting, "I love you!"

From an empty tomb, near Golgotha, from which Christ arose from the dead, God was shouting, "I love you!"

And even now, from these small pieces of bread representing the body of Christ, and from these small cups representing the blood of Christ, each and every Lord's Day, God is still shouting, "I love you!"

As you put that bread into your mouth, and take the cup to your lips, remember that God sent His Son into the world once to take away your sin. He will send Him again to take you home. From the glories of Heaven, God is still shouting, "I love you!"

—Donald R. Revis
Hubbard, Ohio

Date used: _____

# Spiritual Feast

*John 6:48-51*

As is our "habit," we are observing the Lord's Supper on this Lord's Day. In the congregation where I worship, it is our "habit" to observe the Lord's Supper on each Lord's Day.

Did I shock you when I said "habit"? Well, I believe our lives are made up of habits—good and bad. We need to increase the good habits in our lives, and eliminate the bad as much as possible.

Also, I believe our regular observance of the Lord's Supper is a good "habit" (or custom). But, of course, I surely hope it is more than that to most of us!

I hope it is an "act of obedience" to Jesus' command—"Do this in remembrance of me."

I hope it is an "act of remembrance"— remembering His great sacrifice on the cross so that our sins might be forgiven.

I hope it is an "act of worship" of Him who is our Lord and Savior.

I hope it is an "act of confession" of sin and petition for forgiveness.

I hope it is an "act of rededication" of our lives—to live for Him who died for us.

I hope it is a "fulfilling spiritual feast" for us so that we may grow in our spiritual life.

Jesus said, "I am the bread of life. Your forefathers ate the manna in the desert, yet they died. But here is the bread that comes down from heaven, which a man may eat and not die. I am the living bread that came down from heaven. If any one eats of this bread, he will live forever. This bread is my flesh, which I will give for the life of the world" (John 6:48-51).

—Lloyd R. Sparks
Peoria, Arizona

Date used: _____

# Facets of a Diamond

*John 6:53-56*

It is peculiar that the Lord's Supper has been given various names. One reason for this may have to do with various impressions the Lord's Supper has on people. For some, the Lord's Supper impresses upon them to be thankful. For others, the Lord's Supper brings them to a time of renewal and commitment. For some people, the Lord's Supper is a communion with their Savior.

In a way, looking at the Lord's Supper is like looking at a diamond. No matter from which angle you look at it, there is always something of beauty and meaning. Consider some of the names given to this event:

*Communion:* It is called the Communion because, when we participate in it, we are having communion with Christ, and with His people, the church.

*Sacrament:* It is called a sacrament (which has to do with being a *sign* and *oath*). It is an outward sign of an inward spiritual grace and an oath, because through the participation of it we are committing our lives to the Lord.

*Lord's Supper:* It is rightfully called the "Lord's Supper" because it is a supper. It is a spiritual supper which is provided to us by our Lord Jesus.

"Jesus said to them, 'I tell you the truth, unless you eat the flesh of the Son of Man and drink his blood, you have no life in you. Whoever eats my flesh and drinks my blood has eternal life, and I will raise him up at the last day. For my flesh is real food and my blood is real drink. Whoever eats my flesh and drinks my blood remains in me, and I in him'" (John 6:53-56).

Like food that sustains our physical bodies, so Christ's supper sustains us spiritually.

*Eucharist:* It is called a *Eucharist* (which means giving of thanks or gratitude). Christ, in the institution of it, gave thanks. We, in participation of it, give thanks. We give thanks for Christ's sacrifice of His body and blood, and for the salvation this brought us.

I have heard it argued that taking the Lord's Supper each week can be repetitious and can cause it to lose its meaning. However, like a treasured diamond whose facets of beauty are never monotonous, so the Lord's Supper will always be beautiful to those who treasure Christ in their hearts.

—Joe Michael Poynter
Bullhead City, Arizona

Date used: _____

# Weekly and Weakly

*John 14:15-21*

We meet around the Lord's table weekly. The table is spread on the first day of every week, the day when the Lord's people gather for worship.

The Scriptures tell us that the early church met regularly on the first day of the week, and one of the main focuses of their worship was the breaking of bread—participation in the Lord's Supper. The Communion serves as a constant reminder of Jesus' love for us. He allowed His body to be sacrificed and His blood spilled on our behalf. We who are so prone to forget need this regular reminder, and so we meet weekly around the table.

But we also meet *weakly* around the Lord's table; we meet w-e-a-k-l-y here. Perhaps here more than at any other time we know our own frailty. Our lives seem so weak when compared to Jesus' life. Our sin seems to stand out the more. The smallness of our faith is more obvious because here we are so close to Him.

Such weakness should not discourage us. Indeed, it is when we are weak that our Heavenly Father's strength may come to us. When we are most vulnerable, God is most present. Only when we acknowledge our smallness can we truly acknowledge His greatness. Only in humility can this supper really benefit us.

May we meet w-e-e-k-l-y, continually to be reminded of His sacrifice. And may we meet w-e-a-k-l-y, and in Christ find strength. Let's meet Him at His table.

—Frank Musgrave
Harrisburg, Oregon

Date used: _____

# Forgetting the Anguish Because of the Joy

*John 16:20-22*

During the Last Supper, Jesus comforted His disciples about His coming death with these words: "You will grieve, but your grief will turn to joy. A woman giving birth to a child has pain because her time has come; but when her baby is born she forgets the anguish because of her joy that a child is born into the world. So with you: Now is your time of grief, but I will see you again and you will rejoice, and no one will take away your joy" (John 16:20-22).

The disciples did see Him again, after His resurrection. But what about today, for us who have not seen His physical body after the resurrection? First Peter 1:8, 9 reads "Though you have not seen him, you love him; and even though you do not see him now, you believe in him and are filled with an inexpressible and glorious joy, for you are receiving the goal of your faith, the salvation of your souls."

From the New Testament we learn that Jesus Christ is the firstborn from among the dead and the firstborn over all creation. "For by him all things were created . . . He is before all things, and in him all things hold together" (Colossians 1:16, 17).

When we silently pray as we partake at His table, what does the Lord hear? Do you think He hears us praying for forgiveness over yesterday's sins, asking Him for help in certain matters in our lives, or anguishing over why He had to suffer so much for us on the cross?

Do we let Him hear our joy? Does He hear our joy because Jesus Christ is the firstborn over all creation, because He has made us a chosen people, a royal priesthood, a holy nation, a people belonging to God, because we, even though we were dead in our transgressions, have been made alive in Christ?

For this Lord's table, consider in a new way the comforting words our Lord Jesus Christ spoke to His disciples during the Last Supper. For this Lord's table, let us rejoice because we do believe in Him, because we are receiving the goal of our faith; and let us forget the anguish because of our joy that fills us, the joy He promised *no one* will take away, the inexpressible and glorious joy.

—Robert Alan Jacoby
Louisville, Kentucky

Date used: _____

# Much in Common

*Acts 2:42-46*

As the early Christians were together and had everything in common (Acts 2:44), so too, do we have much in common with one another. Sadly, however, often times those things which we hold so dear have become not only common but commonplace. One such item is the gathering of God's people around the Lord's table.

Each week, as brethren, we should come together to remember what our Lord has done, is doing, and will do on behalf of His people. But instead, to some the Lord's Supper is viewed as nothing more than a filler in the morning worship service. We fail to give much though to its implications and relevance.

The gathering of God's people around the table of Christ is the primary reason why we come together. No other aspect of a worship service takes precedence over our communing with our Lord and Savior, Jesus.

The apostle Paul encouraged the Corinthian brethren to each one examine himself "before he eats of the bread and drinks of the cup" (1 Corinthians 11:28). We must examine ourselves and view this all-important time as an opportunity to be renewed in spirit and strengthened in faith.

The Lord's Supper should have an impact in the life of the believer every time it is celebrated. We must not minimize its importance in our Christian experience and daily living.

In the first-century church the Lord's Supper was an integral part of the *agape* or love feast. It was during this time when believers devoted themselves "to the breaking of bread" as they "ate together with glad and sincere hearts" (Acts 2:42, 46). Today, we need to reassert this pattern and idea by observing the Lord's Supper as the climax of why we come together each week.

—Scott A. Brown
Wilkes-Barre, Pennsylvania

Date used: _____

# The Unifying Power of the Blood

*Acts 17:26*

All humans belong to the one distinct body in creation as proven by blood transfusions which cross all racial lines. God has made of one blood all nations of men who dwell on the face of the earth (Acts 17:26). Life is in the blood (Leviticus 17:14). We belong to the same body in creation.

All Christians belong to one distinct body in their redemption. In the upper room Jesus took bread and said, "'Take and eat; this is my body.' Then he took the cup, gave thanks and offered it to them, . . . 'Drink from it, all of you. This is my blood of the covenant, which is poured out for many for the forgiveness of sins'" (Matthew 26:26-28).

Our redemption life is in the blood of Jesus. Through His blood we all belong to the same distinct body, the church of Christ. This crosses all racial and national barriers.

It is a unifying factor where the Lord's table is being observed scripturally and spiritually.

Just as the blood of Jesus provides forgiveness without partiality (for we are all saved by grace), so this table brings us together with meekness and confession and praise. There is no room here for the critic, the contentious, the carnal. Here we acknowledge our needs, confess our unworthiness, and unite with thanksgiving for the blood that gives life and for the body that unites us in Christ Jesus.

—E. L. Russell
Grant, Michigan

Date used: _____

# Christt Died for Us

*Romans 5:7-9*

It was the year 33 A.D. I was part of a mob that stood before Pilate's palace. The Roman soldiers brought out two Jewish prisoners. Pointing to one, Pilate asked, "What shall I do with this man called Jesus?" I shouted along with the rest of the mob, "Crucify Him, crucify Him!"

I stood along a street in Jerusalem, railing and jeering as Roman soldiers led this man Jesus toward Golgotha's hill, forcing Him to bear a heavy wooden cross. On the hill, I watched as they nailed Jesus to the cross, lifting Him up so all could see Him.

With others, I shouted, "If thou be the Son of God, come down from the cross." I gazed upon Him as He writhed in agony. Finally, with a loud voice He cried out, "It is finished," and gave up the ghost. Darkness settled over the place. It began to thunder and lightning.

Then I awoke. This dream made me realize more fully what the apostle Paul later wrote to the Roman Christians, "Very rarely will anyone die for a righteous man, though for a good man someone might possibly dare to die. But God demonstrates his own love for us in this: While we were still sinners, Christ died for us. Since we have now been justified by his blood, how much more shall we be saved from God's wrath through him!" (Romans 5:7-9).

I was a sinner, alienated from God. My sins sent Jesus to the cross. Only because of His sacrifice, am I able to escape the consequences of my sins. My heart cries out in gratitude for what Jesus did for me. What about yours?

—Robert McWaters
Crookston, Minnesota

Date used: _____

# Unity

*1 Corinthians 11:20-29*

The apostle Paul outlines some of the problems in the Corinthian church. They were carrying in food for a "weekly love feast" and, within this framework, Communion services were held. The rich brought plenty and ate it while the poor stood around hungry. Since we are all a part of the body of Christ, Paul said this caused division at the Lord's table—the very place where we should show *unity.*

Anyone who partakes of the Lord's Supper without recognizing Christ's body brings judgment upon himself. We need vertical and horizontal vision. We should look up to the body of Christ on the cross, and we should look to our right and our left, to our Christian brothers and sisters, as the body of Christ (the church).

The Lord's table is not the place for harboring grudges, jealousy, or hatred for fellow Christians. These indicate that we do not love the *whole* body of Christ. To partake of the Lord's Supper with love for Christ but without love for one another is to violate the significance of the Lord's table.

For some, this may be just a religious ritual they take for granted. However, the Lord's Supper is holy and is taken on "holy ground." Our attitude is important. We ought to examine ourselves before we eat the bread or drink the cup. We are partaking of a family meal for the glory of God and the remembrance of His Son on the cross.

—James R. Pleasant, Jr.
Cerulean, Kentucky

Date used: _____

# Let Us Remember

*1 Corinthians 11:23-26*

"The Lord Jesus, on the night he was betrayed, took bread, and when he had given thanks, he broke it and said, 'This is my body, which is for you; do this in remembrance of me.' In the same way, after supper he took the cup, saying, 'This cup is the new covenant in my blood; do this, whenever you drink it, in remembrance of me.' For whenever you eat this bread and drink this cup, you proclaim the Lord's death until he comes" (1 Corinthians 11:23-26).

Each Lord's Day we come to this time of gathering around the Lord's table as He commanded. We remember Him and the sacrifice He made on Calvary for our salvation.

As we do so the question arises, "Just what do we remember about Him?" Do we think only of His shame and suffering? Do we remember Him only as dead and defeated, still hanging on the cross? Must we always picture Him as the disciples placed His lifeless form in the grave?

We should recall that total sacrifice for our benefit, but our thoughts and thanksgiving need not stop there. Let us also remind ourselves that He did not leave us with a spirit of fear. "For God did not give us a spirit of timidity, but a spirit of power, of love and of self-discipline" (2 Timothy 1:7).

Let us appreciate the fact that we serve a risen Savior, not some dead hero. We need not consider alone the humiliation of the trial, but must remember the power of the resurrection. In that way, we can let the joy of the ascension overshadow the sorrow of the crucifixion. The light of His triumph can dispel the darkness of the betrayal. The sorrow of His death should be replaced by rejoicing over eternal life.

We need not walk in a poverty of spirit but can rejoice in our remembrance and appreciation of His triumph over sin and death.

We are thankful that we are privileged to gather at this table with others of like faith and to remember the gift Jesus Christ made to us through His death, burial, and resurrection. May we receive strength from the act of partaking of these emblems and show forth the glory of that gift through the coming week.

—Elsie E. Howard-Meeds
Columbus, Kansas

Date used: _____

# A Memorial

*1 Corinthians 11:23-26*

When I was very young I experienced a disturbing sorrow when my Grandpa Stafford, who made his home with us, died. I was devastated at this loss. Shortly before he died, my Aunt Maude came to stay with us, to help Mother with the housework and care for Grandpa. While visiting us she crocheted a lovely border for a piano scarf, a simple but lovely item that we used for many years before it was stored away. Eventually I inherited it.

Recently I got it out of storage and decided to put it on the piano at the church where I worship. As an heirloom stored away in a drawer it served no purpose but to take up space. Now it serves two purposes: it decorates the piano, thus adding to the beauty of the worship area; it also serves as a reminder of the time Grandpa died.

Communion has two purposes: to serve

as a beautiful, quiet interlude in the worship service and, more importantly, to serve as a reminder of Christ's death for us.

To other worshipers, the piano scarf is probably not even noticed. It is merely part of the beauty of our simple house of worship. But when I see the scarf I am reminded of Grandpa's death, and of Aunt Maude's devotion to her sister and father.

To some worshipers, the Communion service may just be a "nice" interlude in the worship hour. But to the devout Christian the Communion service is much more. It is a time to remember Christ's devotion and His death.

Is the Communion just something that is "stored away" to be observed when convenient? Or is it so important that you must partake weekly, to remember His devotion and His death for us?

—Iola Harris Irwin
Trego, Wisconsin

Date used: _____

# We Thank You

*1 Corinthians 11:24-26*

Lord, it's not easy for us to sit at Your table—I mean, to really sit at it. We can picture You surrounded by the men You loved so deeply. But us? No, Lord. That's not easy. We're not worthy—and yet, You tell us You died to make us worthy. But to hear Your blessing for the bread and the wine? To touch the bread You touched? To drink from the cup that touched Your lips?

Lord, we're there. We're Judas and Thomas and Peter and John—all in one. We've betrayed You. We've doubted You. We've denied You. And we've loved You. Yes, we're there. Thank You for giving us Your body. We partake of this bread in remembrance of You. And the cup—your blood of the New Agreement—we partake of it, too, knowing full well the price You paid—so that we the Judases, the Thomases, the Peters, and the Johns might never know the wrath of God, but instead His grace, His love, and His pardon.

The Scripture says: "And Jesus gave thanks."

Let the record show His people give thanks. Thank You, Jesus.

—C. Norman Noble
Renton, Washington

Date used: _____

# Solemn Joy

*1 Corinthians 11:26*

Have you ever looked around the church during Communion? Do you feel like you are at a funeral and at any moment wailing is about to break out?

At every church I have attended, Communion seems to be a time for mourning. Have we taken the passage in 1 Corinthians 11:26 in the wrong way? "For whenever you eat this bread and drink this cup, you proclaim the Lord's death until he comes."

When we proclaim the Lord's death, are we only contemplating Jesus hanging on the cross? If so, we are doing a grave injustice to Jesus! His death brought victory over death. Along with His death came His resurrection.

Communion should be a time of solemn joy. Yes, let us remember that Jesus died for us, but we must also remember that He is alive today and that death no longer has any meaning over those who are in Him!

Please don't get too upset if you see people quietly smiling during Communion.
They may simply be rejoicing at Christ's
death and resurrection.

—Robert J. Spurgeon
Monrovia, California

Date used: _____

# Until He Comes

*1 Corinthians 11:26*

"For whenever you eat this bread and drink this cup, you proclaim the Lord's death until he comes" (1 Corinthians 11:26).

We read this verse often when we share Communion, and we proclaim the Lord's death by reminding each other of the suffering, the sacrifice, and the great price Jesus paid to take away our sins.

But there is more of that verse worth our consideration. Paul teaches that when we eat and drink, we proclaim His death until he comes. We often overlook these three words. What they say is repeated many times in Scripture. He is coming! This is precisely what gives meaning to His death, and to what we do when we celebrate the Lord's Supper. If He is not coming we are wasting our time. But we are not wasting our time. He is coming!

When we share the bread and the cup, we

are reminded that our Lord is coming again. This is our blessed hope, as we look forward to the day when He shall come, "For the grace of God that brings salvation has appeared to all men. It teaches us to say 'No' to ungodliness and worldly passions, and to live self-controlled, upright and godly lives in this present age, while we wait for the blessed hope—the glorious appearing of our great God and Savior, Jesus Christ" (Titus 2:11-13).

"Since, then, you have been raised with Christ, set your hearts on things above, where Christ is seated at the right hand of God. Set your minds on things above, not on earthly things. . . . When Christ, who is your life, appears, then you also will appear with him in glory" (Colossians 3:1, 2, 4).

What Jesus did at Calvary, He did once for all time. What He does when He comes, He will do once for all eternity.

—Frank Ford
Woodstock, Georgia

Date used: _____

# A Time to Replenish

*1 Corinthians 11:26*

In the high desert of the American south-west, seasons are measured not by temperature and the length of the day as much as by precipitation. Rain is an infrequent occurrence that is limited to only certain times of the year. During the dry season, no clouds break the endless intensity of the sun. Plants cling to their tenuous existence by growing roots far into the dry desert soil to reach pockets of moisture deep below the surface.

Life is given to the desert during the rainy, or "monsoon" season in late summer. A typical day consists of a hot, sunny morning followed by a rapid buildup of clouds at midday. The clouds soon turn dark and open up to produce a brief and often furious thunderstorm.

Suddenly, the dry desert is transformed into infinite channels of running water. Dry stream beds flow at capacity. Most importantly, the underground rivers and lakes that feed the desert are replenished. After the dark clouds deliver their precious treasure, the sky once again clears, only to repeat the drama the next day. Then, as suddenly as it began, the rainy season ends, and long, dry days once again control the life of the desert. In the same way that the rain replenishes the life of the desert, regular Communion with our Lord Jesus Christ rejuvenates the soul of the Christian. As we partake of the elements and "proclaim the Lord's death until he comes" (1 Corinthians 11:26), we are keenly aware of the presence of God and of the inner strength that we draw from the Communion service.

Let us each make the Lord's Supper an opportunity to replenish the deep reservoirs of our faith, so that we may have the living water that we need to make it through our own dry seasons.

—Todd Zeter
Albuquerque, New Mexico

Date used: _____

# Self-Examination

*1 Corinthians 11:28*

We are all familiar with Paul's admonition in 1 Corinthians 11:28 to examine ourselves at Communion time, but how many of us really do?

Self-examination is not an easy task. It's infinitely easier to see faults in other people than it is to see our own faults. It's hard to admit that we have shortcomings and sin in our lives, yet we do.

In 1 John 1:8 we are told, "If we claim to be without sin, we deceive ourselves and the truth is not in us."

If we are not using the Communion time to examine the sin in our lives, we are missing an important benefit of this time in our service. If we come to Communion time thinking we have no sin, we have a real, deep need for self-examination of our Christian commitment.

Self-examination can help us come away

with a renewed desire to be more Christlike, with a better understanding of our weaknesses, and with a deeper appreciation for the infinite grace of God.

We do thank our heavenly Father for His presence in our lives. May we put Jesus' example foremost in our lives this week.

—Wesley Bell
Mesa, Arizona

Date used: _____

# Christ's Healing

*Galatians 2:20*

"I have been crucified with Christ and I no longer live, but Christ lives in me. The life I live in the body, I live by faith in the Son of God, who loved me and gave himself for me" (Galatians 2:20).

How can we be crucified with Christ and still live? Paul says that it is Christ inside him who lives. His fleshly body is propped up, held together, by faith. How is this possible?

Witness a great contrast in the Gospels. A parade of people came to Jesus asking for healing. Two blind men asked for sight, and Jesus asked them, "Do you believe I can do it?" They said yes and were healed because of their faith. A woman sick for twelve years reached out for His coat, and Jesus said, "Your faith has healed you."

But next consider another parade of people who said they wanted to follow Jesus. One wanted to bury his father first; another wanted to say good-bye to his family; another wanted to hold on to all his possessions. Each seeker meant well, but Jesus said they had the wrong priorities.

The first group needed healing of the body and knew it. The second group needed healing of the soul but didn't know it. Yet not one of them could heal themselves.

Healing and redemption cannot be separated. A paralyzed man was lowered through a roof to Jesus. Jesus marveled at his faith and forgave his sins. To the complainers, Jesus responded, "Which is easier: to say, 'Your sins are forgiven,' or to say, 'Get up and walk'?" (Matthew 9:5). Of course, both statements are easy to say, but only the Son of God can do both.

Christ came to bring life and healing during the time of His ministry on earth. Through the cross, He spread that healing across all humanity and all time. Our diseases of both body and soul have been nailed to the cross. Because of the cross we are continually healed by Christ's spirit living in us. This is how we can, as Paul says, be crucified with Christ and still live.

—Daniel C. Massey
Houston, Texas

Date used: _____

# Both Sides of the Cross

*Ephesians 2:11-22*

My visits to the Berlin Wall have been moving experiences. Just before my third visit in 1989 the wall was opened, leading to its eventual dismantling. Experiencing that unique moment in history was exciting, but my most significant spiritual memory resulted from a 1977 visit.

The wall was a symbol of division and despair: divided families, a divided nation, a divided world. In the western sector near Checkpoint Charlie stood a cross, a memorial to a young man shot to death on the other side trying to escape to freedom.

To the Christian that cross was a much more significant memorial. The cross was where Jesus' sacrifice broke down the wall between man and God, and between man and man (Ephesians 2). Because of the cross, life can have a new hope and meaning.

A closer look at the wooden memorial cross in Berlin taught even more. On each side of the cross was a concrete flower pot, insignificant until I noticed that in one pot there was only dirt, a sign of lifelessness, while the pot on the other side of the cross was overflowing with flowers, a picture of life.

71

We must never forget, the cross is not where the gospel story ends. It is followed by a glorious resurrection to life, so we can have hope.

After the crucifixion, the fearful disciples of Jesus were in a state of despair similar to that of people who once looked at the Berlin Wall from the East and realized they might never go beyond it. Yet Sunday came, Jesus was risen, and there was hope for the ages despite walls and barriers in this life.

Our time around the Lord's table should cause us to look to the past: the brutal death of a sinless man dying as a sacrifice for our sins. We should honestly evaluate our personal sins, the grief they cause God and the lifeless condition they bring to us.

Yet it must also be a time to look forward. The crucifixion account does not end in defeat. Jesus' death paid our ransom. That is good news. Then to seal that victory Jesus overcame death itself. He is alive and is coming back! The memorial table anticipates that glorious return. Let's look at both sides of the cross. Let's look intently at the one suffering on the cross. Then let's look at how He wants us to live, and resolve to do it.

—Tom Claibourne
Winchester, Ohio

Date used: _____

# Forgiveness

*Philippians 2:5-8*

"Your attitude should be the same as that of Christ Jesus: Who, being in very nature God, did not consider equality with God something to be grasped, but made himself nothing, taking the very nature of a servant, being made in human likeness. And being found in appearance as a man, he humbled himself and became obedient to death—even death on a cross!" (Philippians 2:5-8).

Every Christian knows that Jesus died on the cross for Christians. His death, burial, and resurrection made it possible for each one of us to have eternal life. What makes His death so special, is that He also died for those who crucified Him. As He hung on the cross, beaten, bleeding, and dying, He still asked God to forgive His persecutors.

Obtaining forgiveness of our sins is a basic element of being a Christian. On the Day of Pentecost, Peter was asked by the

73

people what they should do to be saved. He told them, "Repent and be baptized . . . for the forgiveness of your sins" (Acts 2:38). This means that when we are truly repentant, ask God's forgiveness, and are baptized into Christ, our sins become like they never occurred. The most heinous sins we can ever commit are totally erased!

Confession and repentance are part of the reason we meet together around this table each week. First Corinthians 11:28 reads, "A man ought to examine himself before he eats of the bread and drinks of the cup." By examining ourselves, we reflect on the past week's events and ask forgiveness for the sins we have committed.

As we meet around the Lord's table this week, let's make this an opportunity to examine ourselves and ask forgiveness of our sins.

—Terry Hardwick
Charlotte, North Carolina

Date used: _____

# To Him All Majesty Ascribe

*Philippians 2:8-11*

Around the turn of the century, E. P. Scott served India as one of its earliest missionaries. One day while traveling down a country road, Scott was ambushed by a group of vicious tribesmen. They intended to rob and kill him. As they readied their spears for the attack, Scott abruptly pulled a violin out of his luggage and began playing and singing, "All Hail the Power of Jesus' Name."

The assailants stood motionless as they listened to the message of Jesus in Scott's song. And then he sang, "Let every kindred, every tribe . . . to Him all majesty ascribe." At those words the spears were lowered. As the spears began to drop, one by one, from their hands, some of the would-be murders even began to cry.

The Lord's Supper is an emotional point along life's road when people of every kindred and tribe lay down their arms to ascribe all majesty to Jesus. Here intentions are altered, the course of lives are redirected. At the Lord's Supper men and women of every kind and class drop all thoughts of aggression, possession, and depression to hail Him who saves us by His grace and crown Him Lord of all.

"And being found in appearance as a man, he humbled himself and became obedient to death—even death on a cross! Therefore God exalted him to the highest place and gave him the name that is above every name, that at the name of Jesus every knee should bow, . . . and every tongue confess that Jesus Christ is Lord, to the glory of God the Father" (Philippians 2:8-11).

—Tom Goodlet
Newport News, Virginia

Date used: _____

# "If It's Broken, Fix It"

*Hebrews 4:15, 16*

Have you ever heard the saying, "If it ain't broke, don't fix it"? This usually isn't too difficult for us to accept. What's harder is for us to get something fixed when it's broken. We have a long list of favorite excuses such as:

I've taken it for an estimate, and it'll cost too much.

It's so old they don't make the parts anymore.

I tried to fix it myself, and now it's beyond repair.

I'll just find another one at a garage sale.

I've already had the stupid thing fixed four times.

Sound familiar? We wait until there is extra money or until something dies completely. We wait till a little inconvenience becomes a major hazard. Just as we put off fixing our cars and appliances, going to the dentist, or sewing on that missing shirt button, we often put off matters of the heart and soul. We need to be reminded of Christ's ability to assist us:

"For we do not have a high priest who is unable to sympathize with our weaknesses, but we have one who has been tempted in every way, just as we are—yet was without sin. Let us then approach the throne of grace with confidence, so that we may receive mercy and find grace to help us in our time of need" (Hebrews 4:15, 16).

As we gather around the Communion table, let us thank our Lord Jesus for becoming our high priest through His obedience on the cross.

We can, with confidence, ask God to help us set aside the excuses.

Our Lord knows the hurts, aggravations, temptations, and weaknesses in our lives. He sees when our relationships are broken and when we make a mess of things in an effort to fix them ourselves. Still, He is waiting to help make repairs in our lives so we can better serve Him.

—C. M. Johnson
Porterville, California

Date used: _____

# Hope

*Hebrews 6:11, 19*

The book of Hebrews is full of wonderful spiritual illustrations. One in particular has caught my attention.

Hebrews 6:11, 19 reads: "We want each of you to show this same diligence to the very end, in order to make your hope sure. . . . We have this hope as an anchor for the soul, firm and secure."

An anchor for the soul—what a great word picture! This is how hope works in our lives. The job of an anchor is to remain fixed in the seabed whatever the conditions. In fact, the rougher the weather, the more important the anchor is to the stability and safety of the boat.

To continue the analogy, there has to be a chain connecting the anchor to the ship. Communion is one of the links in that chain, along with prayer, fellowship, and the apostles' doctrine.

Each week as we come to the table and celebrate what Jesus has done for us, we tug on that chain. We are reminded that the anchor is secure, that our hope is steadfast! If we have drifted during the week and there is slack in the line, we can pull ourselves back into close proximity to the anchor.

I don't know about you, but I've gone through some foul weather recently, and I need that anchor in my life.

—James Ricketts
Seaside, Oregon

Date used: _____

# Free

*1 Peter 1:13*

"Buy a new car and get *free* tilt steering."

"Come out to see our lakefront property and get a *free* gift."

"You are already a winner, just call our office and we'll send someone out with your *free* prize."

In today's age of marketing, our minds have been programmed to be very skeptical of the word "free." I'm not sure about you, but when I received my letter in the mail from Ed McMahon, stating that I could be the next millionaire, I didn't run to the phone to call my boss to resign. We have been forced to develop a skeptical nature.

This was really evident to me years ago when I worked in the cable TV industry. When cable was new to an area, they would offer free installation. After time, people came to feel this was no big deal. They even felt the cable company was ripping them off by charging for it. This presented a real problem for the cable companies.

"How can we show people the cost that is involved?" they would say. "We have trucks to buy and maintain, employees to pay, cables to buy, and those trucks use gas. How can we show people that, even though it is free to them, it still has a cost to us?"

At this time in our service, we want to make sure we remember the cost of God's free gift of grace to us. The cable company was not sure how to remind people of the cost for "free" installation.

Jesus did know. He said, "This do in remembrance of me."

We must always remember that grace is a free gift to us, but it wasn't free to God. It was bought with a great price.

—T. L. "Timmy" Farris
Florissant, Missouri

Date used: _____

# The Threefold Look

*Revelation 22:20*

When we come to the Lord's table, we need to take a threefold look.

First, we look back to the cross. We are reminded of His sacrifice, how He gave himself unselfishly and completely, to atone for our sins. The marvelous thing about this is that He did this "while we were still sinners" (Romans 5:8). It has been said, "It is easy to love the lovable, but so hard to love the unlovely."

The second look is to the present—here and now. We look at ourselves: what do we see? What are we doing with our lives? How are we living? Are we striving for holiness? Do we put Jesus first in our lives, or does He come in a poor third? Let us truly examine ourselves, look deep into our hearts (1 Corinthians 11:28, 29). God wants us to acknowledge our sins and humbly ask for forgiveness.

The third look is to the future. Are we looking forward to the time when we will have Communion with our Lord in His kingdom? (Matthew 26:29; 1 Corinthians 11:26). Are we looking forward to His coming with joy or with fear? Someone once asked Dwight L. Moody, "If you knew the Lord would return tonight, how would you spend the rest of the day?" Mr. Moody replied without hesitation, "I wouldn't do anything different than I do every day."

How wonderful if we all could say that! Then we could, with confidence, pray, "Come, Lord Jesus!" (Revelation 22:20).

—Chlo Lillie
Colorado Springs, Colorado

Date used: _____

# New Year's Day

## New Year

*2 Peter 1:19-21*

The Pope will negotiate a peace settlement in Northern Ireland. Cures will be found for three dreaded diseases. Archaeologists in Egypt will find a space ship that crashed in ancient times. The United States will capture aliens from outer space.

Barbara Walters will quit her television career. Grace Kelly will quit her marriage, return to Hollywood, and win an Oscar. Ethel Kennedy will marry Andy Williams.

A rush-hour train will collide with a chemical-laden freight train and hundreds will be killed in America's worst rail accident. Geologists will discover the world's greatest oil reserves under the Great Lakes.

The statements above were predictions made by prominent psychics at the beginning of the year 1977. Similar predictions have been made at the start of every year since then. They have become a staple item in New Year editions of many publications. Despite the failure of psychics to adequately predict the future, millions of people still cling to their every word, article, and column.

Today, however, we celebrate prophecy fulfilled. As the Old Testament prophets foretold, Jesus was born, lived, died, and was resurrected that we might have eternal life.

While many in the non-Christian world still seek—we have found.

As we partake of the body and the blood let us be mindful of the love God had for us as He gave us His Son.

—Rod Irvin
Kingsport, Tennessee

Date used: _____

# New Year's Day

## Everything Old Is New Again

*Hebrews 9:15*

"'The time is coming,' declares the Lord, 'when I will make a new covenant with the house of Israel and with the house of Judah'" (Jeremiah 31:31).

"In the same way, after the supper he took the cup, saying, 'This cup is the new covenant in my flood, which is poured out for you'" (Luke 22:20).

"For this reason Christ is the mediator of a new covenant, that those who are called may receive the promised eternal inheritance—now that he has died as a ransom to set them free from the sins committed under the first covenant" (Hebrews 9:15).

There is an old secular song, "Everything Old Is New Again."

We traditionally look at January 1 as a time to start over again and rid ourselves of old unwise habits, to rid ourselves of extra pounds. In general, we try to get rid of the "old" that is hindering us from being all that we can be, all that God wants us to be.

The new year marks a time to resolve to be and do better with our lives. We resolve to quit bad habits, to read more and watch TV less, to read our Bibles and pray daily, to lose weight, to exercise, and on and on.

In a sense, "everything old is new again" if we allow it to be so. When we become Christians we put off the old and put on the new; we bury the old self and rise to a new life. Let's think about the new things we need to do in this new year and the old things we need to give up with the old year. Let's think about the new covenant from Jesus Christ, and resolve to serve Him in this year ahead.

—Gene Bricker
Santa Fe, Texas

Date used: _____

# Easter

## Tell Me Again, Lord

*Luke 22:19*

*Tell Me Again, Lord, I Forget* is the title of a small book of poems that I have in my library. The phrase really explains why Jesus instituted the practice of partaking of the loaf and the cup. He knew we would need to be reminded of the price He paid to redeem us from our sins, and we need to be reminded every week.

With the push and shove that many of us encounter each day, sometimes the most important things are neglected, even forgotten. Jesus commanded, "Do this in remembrance of me" (Luke 22:19). Jesus knew our weaknesses then and He knows them now. We should never neglect being around the Lord's table each Lord's Day, in obedience to His command.

Tell me again, Lord, of the blood You shed on Calvary to pay the high cost to save me.

Tell me again, Lord, of the agony You suffered that I might have life, and have it more abundantly! Tell me again, Lord, to see You in my place on that cruel cross, that I might feel that soul-searing pain You endured for my sake!

Then tell me again, Lord, lest I forget, of Your resurrection, that I too, will experience resurrection! Then we will enjoy this memorable meal together in Heaven. Tell me again, Lord, lest I forget!

—Earlene Shirley
Grove, Oklahoma

Date used: _____

# Easter

## Out of Darkness

*Matthew 27:45-54*

For many years I got up at 5:30 A.M. to go to work. I stumbled down a 24-foot hallway in the pitch dark, so as not to awaken my daughters. The switch at the far end of the hallway went bad so I replaced it with one that glows in the dark. I don't stumble down that hallway in darkness any more. There is always a light at the end.

Darkness can be very scary. Probably all of us are somewhat afraid of darkness. But what about *total darkness*? Suppose all the lights in the church went out and the sun quit shining. We would be in total darkness. What would you do?

Matthew 27:45 tells us that on the day Jesus was crucified, from the sixth hour until the ninth hour (9:00 A.M.—12:00 noon), total darkness came over the land.

Roman soldiers were resting on Mount Calvary outside of Jerusalem when this happened. They had worked all night. They had taken this man called Jesus, beaten Him, and nailed Him to a cross. Then total darkness for three hours!

"When the centurion and those with him who were guarding Jesus saw the earthquake and all that had happened, they were terrified, and exclaimed, 'Surely he was the Son of God!'" (Matthew 27:54).

The Bible associates sin with darkness. God sent His Son to die on Calvary that we might be redeemed from our sins. God does not want anyone to live in darkness. The Bible says that Jesus is the light of the world. In Him there is no darkness.

Before Jesus went to Calvary, He instituted the Lord's Supper. It is before us this morning. As we partake of the bread and the cup, we are reminded of the love that Jesus showed for us.

If you are a Christian, there is no excuse for stumbling down a dark hallway or living in darkness. There is always light at the end of the way in the person of Jesus Christ.

Jesus came out of that dark tomb on the third day. His light has shown in the world ever since. Take advantage of that light as we commune with our Lord right now.

—Leon Kendall
Flat Rock, Indiana

Date used: _____

# Easter

## In Remembrance

*1 Corinthians 11:24*

Most of us have either read 1 Corinthians 11:24, or seen it engraved on some Communion table, "Do this in remembrance of me." Few may realize, this is the second time that God on a major occasion, commanded His people to do something "in remembrance of . . ." Both were for the same basic purpose, with the same instructions but of different time and occasion.

In Exodus, after God provided the way and means for His people to be delivered from the slavery of Egypt, He gave specific instructions they were to remember the event by celebrating their preparation with a feast. Once a year, in their homes, they were to reenact their preparation for leaving and their journey. Today, after 3,300 years, Jews still celebrate the Passover as instructed.

Jesus said He didn't do anything without first receiving instruction from the Father.

So, in reality God ordained another Feast of Remembrance. We call it "Communion" or "The Lord's Supper." It has the same purpose—remembering again what God did for His people. He provided the way and means for His people to leave their bondage in slavery to sin and start on their way to their Promised Land. In our case, it is a spiritual deliverance; a one-time event, but ongoing in blessing.

Our Communion reminds us of the cross and Christ's resurrection as we go on our lifetime journey to our Promised Land.

Let us always remember from what we were delivered—via the cross—and what it cost our Father!

—Ben C. Moran
Sun City, Arizona

Date used: _____

# Mother's Day

*John 19:25-27*

Jesus had a mother as each of us do. Let's look at what the Scriptures tell us about Jesus' mother, Mary.

First, after Mary bore Jesus and raised Him from a babe to a young lad of twelve, He became lost on His first visit to Jerusalem with His parents. Although He distinguished himself with the teachers of the law in the temple, He quietly returned with His parents (Luke 2:51).

*Let us, like Mary, ponder in our hearts the wisdom of Jesus as we prepare for Communion.*

As a young man, already started on His mission, Jesus and His disciples accompanied His mother to a wedding. She asked Him for help when the wine ran low.

"'Dear woman, why do you involve me?' Jesus replied. 'My time has not yet come.'"

"His mother said to the servants, 'Do whatever he tells you.'" (John 2:4)—and six large jars of water were turned into wine.

*Let us, like Mary, continue to trust in Jesus, even though His words seem to reprove us.*

Later Mary and Jesus' brothers feared for His safety, and perhaps for His sanity, in the tumult He was causing and the enemies He was making (Matthew 12:46).

*Let us repent of the times we think our decisions are better than His teachings. Let us take His Communion in humility.*

Jesus did what He came to do. His blood was shed on a cross like the Passover lamb's blood was shed and sprinkled on the doorposts. Jesus died that others may live. The Passover was now extended to the whole human race. Even then He remembered His mother (John 19:25).

*Let us remember that Jesus has time for each of us, as He had time for His mother. Let us be comforted in the Communion.*

The crucifixion was over, the body tenderly but hastily washed and prepared for burial by the women. A few days later He had risen, and He appeared to many of them. Jesus was not dead but evermore alive. He told them to wait for even more power, from the Holy Spirit from on high (Acts 1:8, 14).

*Let us join in the family of God which includes the blood relations of Jesus because they also believed in Him. Let us partake so we may drink with Him in the new kingdom of God.*

—Lester LeMay
Tempe, Arizona

Date used: _____

# Memorial Day

## In Memoriam

*John 6:53-58*

I help take care of a family cemetery with many graves. Some are not visibly marked, only appearing on the plat map of the cemetery. Others have huge blocks of granite with family names and dates and sayings cut deeply into the surface. Many are of soft limestone, the carving already fading from legibility. Some have been broken, lost into the grass and soil, no longer fulfilling their purpose.

The cemetery is only a century and a quarter old, yet the people buried there have faded from all remembrance. Even the most expensive stones do not bring these people back into our lives. God's plan is for all earthly things to decay, to crumble, to be destroyed.

Jesus chose perishable items as symbols of his imperishable sacrifice and combined them into a memorial that cannot be destroyed by any force on earth. It is rebuilt every time that it is observed, for His memorial is permanent, constructed solely from the love of God in the hearts of His people.

—David Langston
LaRussell, Missouri

Date used: _____

# A Memorial Day Meditation

*John 10:25-30*

This is the weekend that we pause to give honor to those men and women who have given their lives for the defense of our freedom.

Personally, the notion of Memorial Day has always been a little bit foreign to me. I'm nearly forty years old. I have never had a friend who has been killed in any conflicts. I've never lost a close relative to the war. To me, war and the sacrifice that went with it, were just concepts. Even during the Persian Gulf War, it all seemed so much like a Hollywood movie.

The sacrifice of those soldiers never really hit home with me until a few months ago. I was in Washington, D.C., on business. We went to the Vietnam Memorial. For those of you that haven't been there, it is an awesome sight—58,000 names inscribed on a black wall. You just walk and walk and look and look and wonder how many families were touched by each death.

In fact, there are so many names that a directory is provided in which you can look up a name and then locate it on the wall. Out of curiosity, I looked up the name "Harp" to see if there might be any distant relative's name there.

Much to my surprise, I found several Harps named, one name jumped out at me before all the others. Right there in black and white, I found my full name: Michael Lee Harp. It sent chills through me then. It still does even now.

I noted the location and found "my" name on the wall. As I stood there, I wondered what kind of person this other Michael Harp might have been.

That Michael Harp gave his life so that this Michael Harp could enjoy the freedoms that I take for granted.

Those emotions haunted me for several days. I couldn't put my finger on it, but there was something strangely familiar with the feeling. Then, one Sunday morning, it hit me.

The emotions that I felt when I stood before that wall were the same ones that I feel when I stand before the Communion table. In both cases the gift was given freely, sacrificially, at tremendous cost. Each gift allows me to enjoy freedoms that could never be earned on my own. The strongest similarity may be that we sometimes take them both for granted.

The Vietnam Memorial, and those like it serve to remind us of the sacrifices that have been made for us. And of course, so does the memorial feast that we enjoy each Lord's Day morning.

As you partake this Memorial Day weekend, consider the gift that was so freely given for each of us. Remember that wall of names and the cross of Calvary. It's just as if our names were written on that cross. He died in our place so that we might enjoy the freedom of eternal life with Him.

—Michael L. Harp
Marietta, Georgia

Date used: _____

# Father's Day

## Daddy! You're Home

*Romans 8:15*

"Daddy! You're home!" It is the sweetest exclamation to hear from my son when my husband walks through the door at the end of the workday. His eyes aglow, a bright smile breaking across his face, my son demonstrates excitement unrestrained when he sees his daddy.

It is said that any man can be a father. That role is defined as one who has begotten a child, or fulfilled the role as through adoption. He is the one who is to embody respect, discipline, and formality. But from the joy of a child's relationship comes "Daddy." Daddy is a hero who loves and cherishes us, rewards and exalts us, disciplines and trains us. He is a caretaker whose arms reach out to embrace, hold us close, and bring us warmth and security.

Daddy. In Romans 8:15 Paul explains that by the Spirit we have received sonship and

we can cry out to him "Abba, Father"—
Daddy. Jesus Christ, God's own son, made
that possible for us. By His sacrifice, we do
not have to fear the wrath of an angry God;
rather, we can fix our eyes on our hero—
heavenly Daddy who bids His children to
come close, to be enveloped by His love and
forgiveness, to experience His mercy and
peace, and to come home to Him at the end
of the journey.

—Cynthia Ingram
Glen Burnie, Maryland

Date used: _____

# Independence Day

## Miss Liberty

*Matthew 1:21*

The activities surrounding the centennial celebration of the Statue of Liberty may have become boring to many, however there was one unique fact disclosed during those days the United States honored Miss Liberty. There are broken chains at her feet which represent the broken bonds of slavery and tyranny.

I often get a lump in my throat as I read the poem by Emma Lazarus: "Give me your tired, your poor, your huddled masses yearning to breathe free—the wretched refuse of your teeming shore. Send these, the homeless, tempest tossed, to me."

I find it unique that we gather at this table in remembrance of the one who also stands with outstretched arms inviting those "tired huddled masses" yearning to be free from the bondage of sin. Such memories as these need and deserve regular recognition and meditation as we observe the Lord's Supper.

If those huddled masses shed tears as they looked upon Miss Liberty, we should never be ashamed when tears roll down our cheeks thinking about our Lord!

—William B. Venrick
Lancaster, Ohio

Date used: _____

# Labor Day

*1 Corinthians 11:23-26*

Labor Day weekend provides an extra day off in honor of all working people. Many of you have put in your time and you deserve to be honored for your labors and have earned your rest. Some of us are halfway there—twenty down and twenty to go. Some of us are just beginning our commitment of two-score-plus years in the work force. That's a long time.

Most of us will labor more years than Christ's entire earthly walk. Scripture records maybe a thousand days of Christ's work here on earth.

In those one thousand days He calmed the sea, turned water into wine, made the lame walk, caused the blind to see, cleared the temple, raised the dead, fed 5,000 with five loaves of bread and two fish, healed ten men with leprosy, walked on water, and (if that weren't enough), He had one more job to do. He offered himself to be crucified on a Roman-style cross as a living sacrifice on our behalf. He did that too.

Of course we're here today to say, "Thank You, Lord, for Your job well done," and to honor and praise Him by taking of these emblems. The best part of this Labor Day weekend for me isn't that it is three days long and we don't have work tomorrow; the best part is that Christ's work didn't end on the cross. He continues to work for us right now.

—Mike Rehnberg
Florence, Oregon

Date used: _____

# Thanksgiving

*1 Corinthians 11:23-26*

Communion is an act of celebration—a Christmas, Easter, Memorial Day, Independence Day, and Thanksgiving all rolled into one. It is the Christmas dinner by which we acknowledge Jesus' birth as the beginning of God's way to save us from sin. We remember His sacrificial death and resurrection in the way that Easter does. We declare a Memorial Day that is mindful of Jesus' words and deeds, recall that Jesus gave mankind independence from condemnation under the law. Then we also show thanksgiving for God's blessing through the love that Christ showed for us.

Our act of celebration is a solemn occasion, but it is not intended to be mourning Jesus' suffering as much as considering how His crucifixion was a prelude for His resurrection. We are not to put on the sackcloth of sadness, but to glory in the rich garment of rebirth that we share in Communion, because Christ paid the price for it on the cross.

On the occasion of this banquet, we lay aside our daily concerns and concentrate on the worthiness of our holy host. In His graciousness, He serves us wine of miraculous properties, even as He did in His first miracle at the wedding feast. As it meets our body's essential need for drink, its color brings to mind the blood—the very essence of life—that Jesus willingly poured out for us. He serves us bread, giving our bodies the nourishment from the most basic food—"the staff of life"—reminding us of the body He surrendered for the sake of our souls. As we partake of the fruit of the vine and the bread, we share in the very being of Christ.

Our feast is a faith-keeping fellowship of love for our Lord and for one another in His love for us all. The Lord's Supper tells us, too, that with steadfastness of soul, we will be His guests at yet another banquet in the halls of Heaven.

—Daniel J. Smith
New Carlisle, Ohio

Date used: _____

# Christmas

## Christmas Meditation

*Matthew 26:26-29*

At this special time of the year, it seems so natural for our mind's eye to be fixed upon certain seasonal symbols. It is almost as though we delight in shutting out all other thoughts. We focus on the trees in all their beautiful majestic glory; a certain starry night; the angels bringing words of peace and comfort; and most of all, the Christ at His birth.

As we come around the Communion table, it need not be an abrupt change from the beauty of this Christmas time to the hard cold reality of the end of Christ's life here on earth. Compare the Christmas story with the resurrection story by drawing your attention to the scene as it unfolds, blending Matthew 26 and Luke 22.

After sharing the Last Supper with His disciples, Jesus went out to the Mount of Olives with His disciples following Him.

Perhaps it was a starry night as Jesus asked His young men to keep watch and to pray.

Then, alone, He went about a stone's throw beyond them to also pray to His Heavenly Father. There in the intensity of Jesus' time of prayer, an angel suddenly appeared on the hillside; this time to the Messiah, to bring words of peace and comfort. When Jesus returned to His disciples, He found them asleep like sheep, safe in the presence of the Shepherd.

Of course the story doesn't end there. It goes on to another tree at Calvary. A tree made beautiful only by the majestic body of the King of kings draped upon it. Then, suddenly, before our eyes, unfolded the miraculous rebirth of Jesus. Not from the womb, but from the tomb. The victory of life eternal over death.

May we at this Communion time see in this bread and this cup, the body and the blood of our living Savior. May our sins be forgiven and we be filled with the Holy Spirit as we serve God.

—Walt Mielke
Indianapolis, Indiana

Date used: _____

# Did Joseph Know?

*Matthew 1:18-24*

Triumphant choruses cascade from Heaven welcoming the Creator as He enters the form of His handiwork to save them from themselves. The gifts received, the carols ringing, no one quite realizing what lay ahead for the tiny bundle wrapped in dish towels and dust rags.

I think Joseph must have known something. I think he saw it, as he looked down at the child with all the exuberant wonder a new dad can muster. Knowing in his heart that he was less father than caretaker, yet proud just the same. He probably had visions of wrestling in the living room, junior-carpenter tool belts, and late night father-son talks. But I think he saw it.

He saw the shadow over the stable. Whether he knew exactly what it was, no one knows for sure. He might have seen the shadow of the future and asked, like all fathers, "Will I teach him the right things? Will I tell him enough? Can I really prepare him to be a man?"

He did not know that the shadow over the baby's crib had loomed since the garden. For in spite of all the hope, in spite of all the promise, in spite of all the joy surrounding His birth, this baby was born in the shadow of a cross.

Joseph never saw the cross himself, but on that glorious evening he must have seen its shadow. If he could have known that the child he held was the light that would remove that shadow forever.

As we prepare for this Communion time, let us think of the stable. Let us see the shadow. Let us be awed by the light. "O, come let us adore Him, Christ the Lord."

—Jeff Thackston
Frankfort, Indiana

Date used: _____